You Are Never Alone

Owlkids Books acknowledges the financial support of the Canada Council for the Arts, the Ontario Arts Council, the Government of Canada through the Canada Book Fund (CBF) and the Government of Ontario through the Ontario Creates Book Initiative for our publishing activities.

Published in Canada by
Owlkids Books Inc.
1 Eglinton Avenue East
Toronto, ON M4P 3A1

Published in the United States by
Owlkids Books Inc.
1700 Fourth Street
Berkeley, CA 94710

Library of Congress Control Number: 2018949744

Library and Archives Canada Cataloguing in Publication

Kelsey, Elin, author
    You are never alone / written by Elin Kelsey ; artwork by Soyeon Kim.

ISBN 978-1-77147-315-6 (hardcover)
    1. Human ecology--Juvenile literature. 2. Ecology--Juvenile literature. I. Kim, Soyeon, illustrator II. Title.

GF48.K458 2019   j304.2   C2018-903931-0

Edited by Mary Beth Leatherdale
Designed by Alisa Baldwin

Manufactured in Shenzhen, Guangdong, China, in June 2021, by WKT Co. Ltd.
Job #21CB0793

B   C   D   E   F   G

ONTARIO ARTS COUNCIL
CONSEIL DES ARTS DE L'ONTARIO
an Ontario government agency
un organisme du gouvernement de l'Ontario

Canada Council
for the Arts

Conseil des Arts
du Canada

Canada

Publisher of Chirp, Chickadee and OWL
www.owlkidsbooks.com

Owlkids Books is a division of   bayard canada

A huge thank you to the remarkable team who brought this book to life: Soyeon Kim, Mary Beth Leatherdale, Karen Boersma, and Alisa Baldwin.

You Are Never Alone is dedicated to the more than eight million other species on Earth—along with Esme, Kip, Katherine, James, Matthias, Lucas, Alanna, Fiona, Marielle, Sylvie, Janice, Karen, Alison, Cookie Dough, Zerz, and all the cherished family and friends—who make up my blast radius of love.

—EK

For Eunyoung, Jungmin, and Sooyeon
엄마, 정민이, 아빠, 사랑해!

Thank you with all my heart—Mary Beth Leatherdale, Alisa Baldwin, and Elin Kelsey —for believing in me to create the world of You Are Never Alone.

—SK

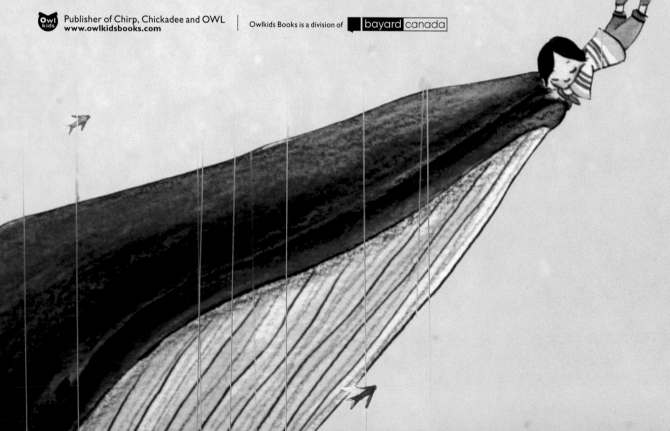

You Are Never Alone

Written by
Elin Kelsey

Artwork by
Soyeon Kim

OWLKIDS BOOKS

Every moment

this beautiful planet

showers you with gifts.

Clouds rain fresh water
to quench your thirst.

Your lungs swell with
oxygen that plants create.

Earthworms, ground beetles,
and ants plow the soil where
your vegetables grow.

Nature touches every bite you eat.

You gobble fruits from plants
pollinated by bats in the twilight
and bees in the day.

Ocean algae thicken
the ice cream you lick.

You devour fish
who ate tiny plankton
fertilized by poop
from whales in the sea.

When danger lurks, help
comes in wild ways.

Mangrove roots hold tight
to slippery mudslides.

Poplar trees drink up floods.

Forests of undersea kelp
calm ferocious waves.

You are protected by
a generous world of green.

Branches stretch across streets,
creating peaceful neighborhoods.

Mother trees
entwine their roots,
raising vast shady forests
that keep you and the planet cool.

You always have company.

Armies of microorganisms
snuggle against your skin,
keeping germs at bay.

Your face is a home
to wee little cleaning mites
who evolved from mites that lived
on the faces of your relatives.

You grow strong
with the help of bacteria that
digest the food in your tummy.

They were passed down
from your mother
when you were born.

If things break,

remember

healing happens, too.

Corals rebuild strong reefs,
just as your bones
mend a fracture.

Aloe vera soothes your itchy skin.

Ginger settles your upset tummy.

Wallowing in the mud
makes you smarter,
thanks to a surge of
feel-good chemicals
triggered by
bacteria in the soil.

You thrive through connections
to the land and the sea.

Whales rise and dive,
splashing phytoplankton to the surface,
where the sun powers their growth.

Krill gobble these ocean plants
and become food for salmon.

Bears drag spawned salmon
onto shore,
spreading fishy nutrients
that help massive trees grow.

Forests maintain
the Earth's climate.

More whales
means more plants
and fish and bears

and a healthier you.

You turn to pets for support,
just as they count on you.

Gaze into your dog's eyes and
you both feel a rush of love.

Just thinking about your cat
soothes lonely times.

You sense these wild connections.

Sunshine fills you with hope.

Your imagination smiles when you climb a tree.

You are never alone.

Feel gravity hug you tight

as you twirl around the sun.

A note from the author

One day, while I was walking with my friend Corbin to his new home (which was farther away from his familiar neighborhood than he wished), he turned to me and said, "It's okay. It's still within the blast radius of love." There was something about that phrase that perfectly captured the wonderful feeling of being part of a community that is always there for you, no matter what. I wrote this book because I want every kid to realize that warm, supportive community already exists for all of us. I want to look every kid in the eye and say, "No matter what is happening in your life, you are never alone. Every plant on Earth creates a bounty of oxygen to fill your lungs. This big beautiful planet is alive, generously creating water, food, air, trees, rainbows, and countless other gifts."

Too often, in our well-intentioned efforts to raise awareness of environmental problems, we leave kids with the idea that the Earth is wrecked and it is up to them to fix it. Environmental issues are real, and many of them are urgent, but all that gloom and doom simply leaves kids feeling worried and hopeless. And it ignores the extraordinary power and resilience of ecosystems all over the planet. All the examples in this book are supported by current science. If you live on a tree-lined street, for example, you'll experience health benefits equal to being seven years younger. When you play in the mud, you ingest tiny bacteria from the soil that help you learn things faster. Gazing into your dog's eyes triggers hormones in you—and your dog—that generate feelings of trust and goodwill toward others. It's the same kind of hormone release that creates the bond between mothers and their babies.

Every time I think of all the plants and animals and earth systems that make it possible for me to lie back in the sunshine without a care in the world, I feel so grateful and lucky, I want to dance a jig. So when you finish reading, I hope you will put this book down, grab the hands of someone you love, and give a gigantic jump for joy as you twirl around the sun.

Warm thoughts,
Elin

P.S. To find out more about the science behind this book, be sure to visit: www.owlkidsbooks.com/youareneveralone.